Sandra Bouquet Carslick
Vicki Norton Remsen

I admire your "grace" in this difficult time ♡ Love – Diane

Lone Lotus Publishing
Camden, Maine

Printed and Published in the USA
Lone Lotus Publishing
P.O. Box 309, Camden, ME 04843
www.lonelotus.com

Cover design: Lauren Watkinson
Photography: Phyllis Giobbi

Library of Congress Control Number: 2011941141

The authors of this book do not dispense medical advice or prescribe the use of any technique as a form of treatment for physical or medical problems without the advice of a physician, either directly or indirectly. The intent of the authors is only to offer information of a general nature to help you in your quest for emotional and spiritual well-being.

Second Edition
1st printing, November 2011
5th printing, September 2015
ISBN-10: 0984683801
ISBN-13: 978-0-9846838-0-2

In This Moment...

the little book of emotions

was created to help you acknowledge and witness your emotions. Acknowledging feelings, without judging them, gives them a voice. Calling upon the pages of this book in times of need will help facilitate the shift that allows you to move forward in this moment.

Suggestions for using

In This Moment...

the little book of emotions

1. Acknowledge the emotion rather than push it away.
2. Find the emotion in ... *the little book of emotions*. Observe the photograph and allow yourself to feel the emotion.
3. Breathe deeply into your belly several times.
4. Read the affirmation accompanying the photograph. Be open to a shift or new possibility as you release the emotion.
5. Appreciate the emotion for the awareness it has provided.

Agitation

I acknowledge I am feeling agitated, and I ask in this moment that this turmoil within me be replaced with calm composure.

Amazement

I acknowledge this great joy and surprise, and ask in this moment that my life always be blessed with wonder.

Anger

I acknowledge the anger I am feeling,
and I ask in this moment for the guidance
to respond with a reasoned attitude.

Anxiety

I acknowledge the anxiety I am feeling, and I ask in this moment to slow and expand my breath and allow a sense of calm to infuse my body.

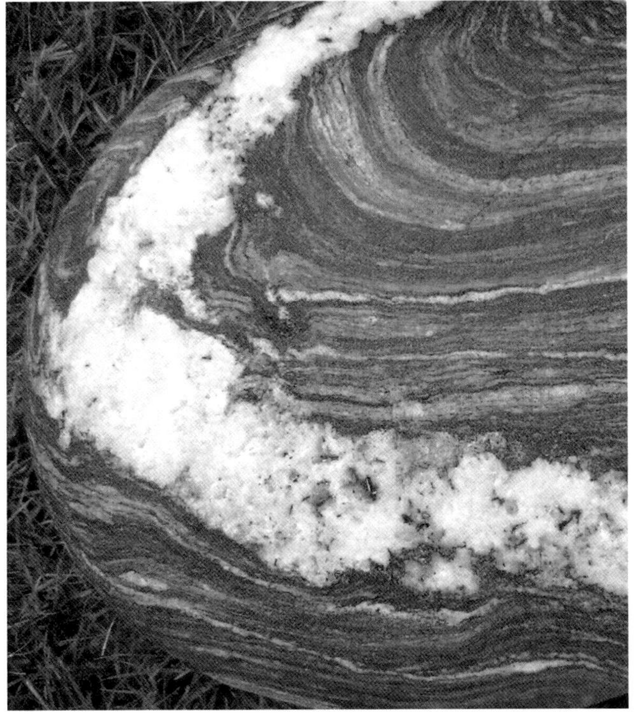

288

Betrayal

I acknowledge the betrayal I am feeling, and I ask in this moment to find the inner resources to face this situation with honesty, clarity, and forgiveness.

Compassion

I acknowledge my need to feel compassion for myself and others, and I ask in this moment to connect in a kind and caring way.

Conflict

I acknowledge the conflict in my life,
and I ask in this moment to be open
to harmony and resolution.

Confusion

I acknowledge the confusion in my life, and I ask in this moment for the gift of clarity and focused awareness.

Courage

I acknowledge my need for courage in this situation, and I ask in this moment for the inner resources to move forward in spite of my fear.

Crisis

I acknowledge my life is in crisis, and I ask in this moment for the insight to know the next best step for me to take right now.

Depression

I acknowledge the depression that has darkened my thoughts, and I ask in this moment to release self-judgment and allow hope to lighten my spirit.

Disappointment

I acknowledge the disappointment I am experiencing, and I ask in this moment to release my expectations so I may feel a sense of peace with the present situation.

Embarrassment

I acknowledge the embarrassment I feel, and I ask in this moment to release the discomfort and humiliation, and regain my sense of confidence.

Emptiness

I acknowledge the emptiness I feel, and I ask in this moment to be filled with a sense of purpose and meaning.

Exhaustion

I acknowledge how exhausted I feel, and I ask in this moment to allow myself the time to rest and re-energize.

Failure

I acknowledge a sense of failure, and I ask in this moment that I remember the many successes that have enriched my life.

Faith

I acknowledge the present situation requires faith, and I ask in this moment to suspend rational thought and trust in my beliefs.

Fear

I acknowledge the fear I am feeling,
and I ask in this moment for the courage
and confidence to face life's challenges.

Forgiveness

I acknowledge the need to forgive, and I ask in this moment to free myself of the burdens of bitterness and resentment.

Frustration

I acknowledge this frustration I am experiencing, and I ask in this moment to regain my perspective and patience and be open to solutions that can ease my irritation with the present situation.

Gratitude

I acknowledge the gratitude I feel,
and I ask in this moment to savor the
blessings each day brings.

Grief

I acknowledge the grief I am feeling, and I ask in this moment for acceptance of what is present in my life now as I invite gentle healing from this pain.

Guidance

I acknowledge my need for guidance, and I ask in this moment for insights and resources that lead me toward the truth.

Guilt

I acknowledge the guilt I am feeling, and I ask in this moment to forgive myself and accept that I am doing the best I can.

Happiness

I acknowledge this feeling of pure happiness, and I am reminded in this moment that happiness is a choice I can always make.

Healing

I acknowledge I need healing, and I ask in this moment that my mind, body, and spirit be open to all forms of healing that will serve my highest good.

Humor

I acknowledge the power of humor, and I ask in this moment to remember that during life's challenges humor can lighten my burdens.

Inspiration

I acknowledge the gift of inspiration, and I ask in this moment that it continue to fuel my passion and feed my soul.

Irritation

I acknowledge the irritation I am feeling, and I ask in this moment to keep life's annoyances in perspective.

Jealousy

I acknowledge the jealousy I feel, and I ask in this moment to let go of judgment, insecurity, and false beliefs I now hold.

Joy

I acknowledge this feeling of joy, and I ask in this moment to recognize and remember those times when joy blesses my life.

Loneliness

I acknowledge the loneliness I feel, and I ask in this moment to embrace this solitude and connect to my inner wisdom.

Love

I acknowledge that love is the most powerful force in the universe, and I ask in this moment to remember that our greatest gift to the world is to give and receive love.

Pain

I acknowledge the pain I feel, whether it be physical or emotional, and I ask in this moment that loving energy fill my being and ease my discomfort.

Panic

I acknowledge the panic I am feeling, and I ask in this moment to stop, breathe, and bring in the feeling of calm that enables me to move forward with confidence.

Patience

I acknowledge my need for patience, and I ask in this moment to be tolerant and understanding of those around me.

Peace

I acknowledge this sense of peace I feel, and I ask in this moment to savor the serenity.

Regret

I acknowledge the regret I feel,
and I ask in this moment to release
the past and move forward with
positive intention.

Rejection

I acknowledge I feel rejection, and I ask in this moment to reframe my perception of disapproval and embrace my true, authentic self.

Resentment

I acknowledge the resentment I feel, and I ask in this moment to release the burden of animosity and focus on forgiveness.

Sadness

I acknowledge this sadness I feel, and
I ask in this moment to release the
tears that can cleanse my spirit.

Self-Acceptance

I acknowledge my need for self-acceptance, and I ask in this moment to remember those practices and rituals that enable me to love and embrace all facets of my unique self.

Self-Confidence

I acknowledge my need for self-confidence, and I ask in this moment to be guided forward with faith, trust, and courage.

Serenity

I acknowledge my need for serenity amidst life's confusion, and I ask in this moment to remember that I can always choose peace.

Shame

I acknowledge the shame I am feeling, and I ask in this moment to release self-judgment and to love and accept myself just as I am.

Sickness

I acknowledge the sickness that has come into my life, and I ask in this moment to be open to healing in all its manifestations.

Stress

I acknowledge the stress I feel, and I ask in this moment to slow down, breathe, and return to a place of balance.

Support

I acknowledge my need for support, and I ask in this moment for the courage to seek help from others and be willing to accept the gifts from those who intend to uplift me.

Surprise

I acknowledge this joyful surprise, and I ask in this moment to embrace life's surprises with child-like wonder.

Surrender

I acknowledge my need to surrender, and I ask in this moment for the grace to let go and accept those things I cannot control.

Trust

I acknowledge trust as a necessary part of life, and I ask in this moment that I rely on my faith, beliefs, and heart-centered wisdom to carry me through.

Turmoil

I acknowledge the turmoil in my life, and I ask in this moment to find the order and harmony that will bring me back into balance.

Wisdom

I acknowledge I am blessed with wisdom, and I ask in this moment to heed my inner voice and trust its guidance.

Worry

I acknowledge the worry burdening my thoughts, and I ask in this moment to release ownership of this issue and trust in a positive outcome.

About the Authors...

At this moment, you may find **Sandra Bouquet Carslick** enjoying life at her home in Brunswick, ME, with her husband, two children and two grandchildren, an adorable grandson and a beautiful new granddaughter. She may also be traveling to Morocco or New Mexico, maybe Arizona, or pedaling her bike around Mid-Coast Maine with a huge smile on her face. When not otherwise exercising, traveling, or writing, she offers Reiki and Reconnective Healing® from her private practice in Brunswick.

Her passion for helping others heal blossomed from her own journey through illness, disability, and pain. Diagnosed with Reflex Sympathetic Dystrophy following a routine surgery, she found she was unable to use her arm or hand and experienced chronic, excruciating pain. She was forced to give up her career as a Radiation Therapist and became bedridden. “I had no place to hide,” she recalls. “I realized I had been living on autopilot and had conveniently tossed my feelings as they rose into my ‘emotional closet’. Lying in bed with nothing to do I was forced to drag them out, one by one, and experience them. It was incredibly painful, but something amazing happened in the process. I began to feel lighter. I began to have less pain. I realized that by acknowledging these emotions and feeling them I was releasing them from my body. I had given myself permission to feel again! I had given myself the gift of awareness.”

This simple little book of emotions was conceived from Sandra’s experience. May it help you on your path to self-awareness and health.

Living near the ocean and walking on the beach is what nourishes **Vicki Norton Remsen**. Every day she is grateful to live on the coast of Maine. When she's not wading in the water, she's gardening, hiking, or visiting care facilities with therapy dogs. "Soft ears and a wagging tail create the biggest smiles. Animals can be so therapeutic and selfless."

After twenty-two years as a teacher, coach, administrator, and college consultant, a neurological injury (focal dystonia) to her right arm abruptly ended Vicki's academic career. She could no longer write. She experienced a number of other significant losses at the same time. "I felt useless, stupid, and defeated, but I put on a happy face and pretended all was just fine. Burying my feelings didn't work very well. I was exhausted and depressed. Traditional medicine couldn't fix me, so I began investigating alternative therapies. Through the study of EFT (Emotional Freedom Technique) and Quantum Touch, I learned about the importance of recognizing and releasing trapped emotions. Through this process I was able to release a lot of negativity and make room for other possibilities in my life, and created a business that provided support and compassionate care for the elderly who wanted to remain in their homes."

"Because I believe our mess can often be our message, I wanted to share with others this gift of empowerment. *The little book of emotions* helps its readers bring their emotions into the light and use them to move forward in their lives."

About the Photographer...

Phyllis Giobbi has a lifetime passion for photography.

As a former travel consultant she was given the opportunity to travel the world, where she captured the essence of each place she visited with her camera.

Since moving to the Maine coast in 1994, Phyllis finds herself surrounded by nature's beauty with an abundance of photographic possibilities.

The photos she is sharing in this book are the raw, unedited, original photos, many of which she captured in the state she now calls her home.

Phyllis may be contacted via email at:
pgiobbiphotos@gmail.com

To order copies of *In This Moment...* the little book of emotions please complete the following:

Please send me ______ copies of *In This Moment...* at $12.95 each. I have enclosed $__________ for book(s), plus $2.50 shipping and handling for 1-2 books, $5.95 for 3-5 books or FREE SHIPPING for 6 or more books for a total of $__________.

Make check payable to Lone Lotus LLC
and mail with this form to:

Lone Lotus LLC
P.O. Box 309
Camden, Maine 04843
1-855-545-2665

Name ______________________________

Address ______________________________

City/State/Zip ______________________________

Phone ______________________________

You may also order online at www.lonelotus.com